Colo Triangula Trade.

An Economy Based on Human Misery

Edited by Phyllis Raybin Emert

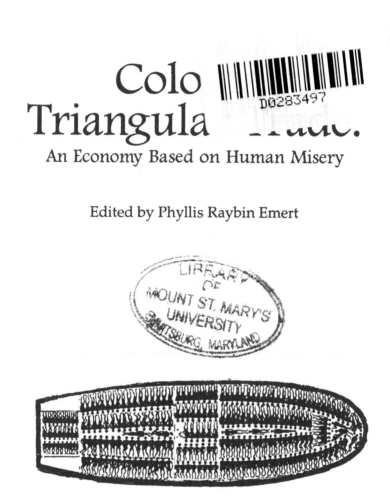

Discovery Enterprises, Ltd.
Carlisle, Massachusetts

© Discovery Enterprises, Ltd., Carlisle, MA 1995
ISBN 978-1-878668-48-6
Library of Congress Catalog Card Number 95-68772

Printed in the United States of America

Dedication

Special Thanks to:
The Libraries of the Claremont Colleges
Claremont, California

Subject Reference Guide

Colonial Triangular Trade: An Economy Based on Human Misery
edited by Phyllis Raybin Emert

Colonial Slave Trade — U.S. History
Slavery — U.S. History
African-American History — History

Photo/Illustration Credits

Cover Illustration, Stowage of the British ship *Brookes* (p. 43),
Taverns and storefronts of 1865 (p. 53), courtesy of the Library of Congress.

Olaudah Equiano (p. 47), courtesy of The New York Historical Society.

Table of Contents

Foreword

Throughout human history, there has always been slavery. Thousands of years ago, ancient civilizations like Babylonia, Assyria, Egypt, Israel, Arabia, Greece and Rome had slaves. The famous Greek philosopher, Aristotle (384-322 B.C.) once said that a slave's life consisted of three things: work, punishment, and food. It was the slaves who toiled in the mines, farmed the plantations, and labored at whatever hard work their owners assigned them.

Most slaves were captured in war or were criminals. This was even the case in Africa, where slavery existed long before the Europeans became involved in the colonial slave trade which began in the 15th century.

Slavery has always been a question of power and economics. Those with money had power and control. Those without money were powerless and controlled by others.

Yet the African triangular slave trade was historically different in two distinctive ways from ancient slavery. First, the majority of the slaves were taken from the West African coast and transported to North and South American colonies for one specific purpose. They provided a lifetime of labor by working on plantations that produced crops like tobacco, sugar, rice, and cotton which were sold for large profits.

Second, unlike the ancient world where color was not an issue and whites enslaved other whites, in the African trade, all slaves were black and all owners were white. Racism, or the idea that blacks, because of the color of their skin, were somehow inferior and less than human, came to be used as a reason or justification for slavery.

This book will focus on the Atlantic slave trade and the colonial triangular trade route in particular. It deals with the profits, the losses, and the harsh brutalities of the slave trade which continued for several centuries into the 1800s. Like it or not, the Atlantic trade contributed to the commercial and economic development of Europe, America, and other New World colonies, and subsequently helped bring about the Industrial Revolution.

At the same time, it had a negative effect on African society and scattered black people throughout the world against their will. It brought about the Civil War in the United States and laid the foundation for racial discrimination. The effects of the Atlantic slave trade are still being dealt with today.

Note: All spelling and grammar in the excerpted selections in this book are reprinted as originally written.

The African Slave Trade

"It was the Portuguese who...started the Atlantic slave trade
and established the first European overseas empire," declared
James Rawley in his book, *The Transatlantic Slave Trade.*

In 1441, explorer Antam Gonsalvez shipped ten black men
from the Northern Guinea coast in Africa back to Portugal as a
gift to Prince Henry. By the end of the 15th century, the Portuguese built a fort on Africa's Gold Coast and the Pope gave
them exclusive rights to the slave trade, which they dominated
for more than a century.

If 1441 marked the beginning of the Atlantic trade, then
1492, the year Christopher Columbus discovered the New
World, was also significant. It was Columbus' discovery that
marked the beginning of the development of New World colonies
by the European powers. These territories, from Brazil in the
south through the West Indies to the American colonies in the
north, required masses of slave labor to promote their agricultural
economies.

Throughout the 16th century, the Portuguese supplied the
Spanish and Portuguese settlements in Central and South
America and the Caribbean with African slaves. It was in 1518
that the first black cargo of slaves, shipped directly from Africa
to the West Indies, was used to work on the sugar plantations.

England showed little interest in the slave trade until Captain
John Hawkins made three voyages to Africa in the mid-16th cen-
tury. Knowing that black slave labor was desired in Hispaniola
(Haiti), Hawkins believed there was money to be made on the
African coast. He loaded up three ships with a cargo of English
goods and set sail in October, 1562.

The Principal Navigations, Voyages, and Discoveries Made by the English Nation

by Richard Hakluyt

(London, 1589, from George Francis Dow, *Slave Ships And Slaving*, Salem, Massachusetts: Marine Research Society, 1927, pp. 20-21).

... hee [Hawkins] passed to Sierra Leona, upon the coast of Guinea, which place by the people of the country is called Tagarin, where he stayed some good time, and got into his possession, partly by the sword and partly by other meanes, to the number of 300 negroes at the least, besides other merchandises, which that Country yeldeth. With this praye he sailed over the Ocean sea unto the Island of Hispaniola, and arrived first at the port of Isabella: and there hee had reasonable utterance of his English commodities, as also of some part of his Negroes, trusting the Spaniards no further than by his owne strength he was able still to master them. From the port of Isabella he went to Porte de Plata, where he made like sales, standing always upon his gard: from thence also hee sailed to Monte Christi; another port on the north side of Hispaniola, and the last place of his touching, where he had peaceable trafique and made vent of the whole number of his Negroes: for which he received in those 3 places, by way of exchange, such quantity of merchandise, that he did not onely lade his owne 3 shippes with hides, ginger, sugers, and some quantitie of pearles, but he fraighted also two other hulkes with hides and other like commodities, which he sent to Spaine. And thus leaving the Island, hee returned and disimboked, passing out by the Islands of the Caycos, without further entring into the Bay of Mexico, in this his first voyage to the West India, and so with prosperous successe and much gaine to himselfe and the aforesaid adventurers, he came home and arrived in the moneth of September 1563.

⚔ ⚔ ⚔ ⚔

This first voyage was so successful that Hawkins made two more trips to the African coast. The second voyage was also very profitable, but the third ended in failure when the Spaniards captured his ships and imprisoned Hawkins' crew.

The English were not active in the slave trade again until the 17th and 18th centuries, yet Hawkins' two successful voyages were the earliest examples of the first triangular trade route. English goods were shipped to Africa for slaves. The slaves were carried to the West Indies and sold for profit. Then the ships returned to England with colonial goods and products bought with the money made from the sale of the slaves.

During the 17th century, nations like Denmark, Holland, Sweden, France, and England became involved in the African slave trade as they acquired colonies in the Caribbean and the Americas. With the development of the sugar industry and the increased demand for laborers, slaves became an essential element for economic success.

The English settled in Bermuda in 1609, St. Christopher in 1623, Barbados in 1625, then the Leeward Islands, Antigua, Montserrat, and the eastern coast of North America by 1632. The French settled in Guadeloupe and Martinique in 1635, Marie Galante in 1648, and St. Lucia and Grenada in the 1650s. The Dutch acquired Curacao, St. Eustatius, and Tobago in the 1630s; and the Danes settled in St. Thomas in 1671.

The English formed the Company of Adventurers of London in 1618 and the Dutch West India Company was established in 1621, both dealing exclusively with the African slave trade.

The first Africans arrived in North America in 1619 at Jamestown, Virginia, one year before the Mayflower arrived in Plymouth, Massachusetts. A Dutch ship sold "twenty Negars" to the colonists. At first, Africans were treated like other indentured servants who were brought from England. They worked for five to seven years and then were given their freedom. But there were not enough indentured servants to meet the demand for labor in

9

the tobacco colonies of Maryland and Virginia. American Indians were not reliable or cooperative workers, so plantation owners turned to black Africans, who, once purchased, were held as slaves for life.

This attitude of perpetual slavery and the obvious racial distinction from whites contributed to the belief over time that blacks were somehow different and less human than other people. By 1660, slavery was written into law in a number of American colonies.

In the New World, slavery was legitimized to meet the labor shortage wherever certain crops, grown for profit, were in demand in Europe. These crops included sugar in the West Indies and Brazil, then tobacco, rice, indigo, and later, cotton, in the southern American colonies. It was a system of labor and economics in which Europeans and then Americans profited.

With the increased demand for sugar and the development of the English West Indian sugar colonies of Barbados and Antigua, the British became very involved in the the African slave trade. They established the Royal African Company in 1672 and their naval superiority allowed them to completely dominate the African trade by the 18th century.

In the middle 1700s, Parliament passed a law allowing free and open trade in Africa. Three British cities emerged to form the backbone of the English slave trade — London, Bristol, and Liverpool. They supplied great numbers of slaves to the Virginia tobacco plantations and to the rice and indigo planters in South Carolina. As the demand for these crops grew, their production became the basis of the American economy. (Cotton became a significant crop towards the end of the century, especially after the development of Eli Whitney's cotton gin in 1763.)

New England entered the slave trade and Newport, Bristol, and Providence, Rhode Island, (and to a lesser extent, Boston and Salem, Massachusetts) emerged as major slaving ports and suppliers of slaves to the West Indies and the southern colonies.

The trade stimulated regional ship-building and the production of rum distilled from sugar and molasses, obtained in trade from the West Indies, which was then used to obtain slaves in Africa.

John Adams, one of America's Founding Fathers and the second President of the United States, once declared, "Molasses was an essential ingredient of American independence."

The African slave trade was nearly three hundred years old by the time the American colonies became active participants. Their involvement, (as well as the involvement of other countries in the trade) had nothing to do with morality, right and wrong, or religious beliefs. It was not an issue of owning other human beings as pieces of property.

It was a matter of business — supply and demand, capital and commerce. The labor shortage, the agricultural economies of the southern colonies, the increasing demand from European markets for New England rum and Southern crops, and the American demand for English and European products, all combined to promote the slave trade — simply because it was a profitable and money-making venture.

———————————

The following excerpts focus mainly on British and American involvement in the African slave trade and its commercial aspects.

Charter of the Royal African Company

(From Elizabeth Donnan, *Documents Illustrative of the History of the Slave Trade to America – Volume I – 1441-1700*. New York: Octagon Books, Inc., pp. 186-7, originally published in 1930).

... We do hereby, for us, our heirs and Successors, grant unto the said Royal African Company of England and their Successors, that it shall and may be lawful to and for the said Company and their Successors, and none others, from time to time to set to Sea such and so many shipps... as shall be thought fitting by the said Court of Assistants for the time being, of [which] the Governor, Sub-Governor, or Deputy Governor to be one prepared and furnished with Ordnance, Artillery and Ammunition or any other habiliments in warlike manner fitt and necessary for their defence; And shall for ever hereafter have, use and enjoy all mines of Gold and Silver ... And the whole, entire and only Trade, liberty, use and privilege of Trade and Traffic into and from the said parts of Africa ... into and from all and singular Regions, Countries, Dominions, Territories, Continents, Islands, Coasts and places now or at any time heretofore called or known by the name or names of South Barbary, Guinny, Buiny or Angola or any of them ... for the buying, selling, bartering and exchanging of, for, or with any Gold, Silver, Negroes, Slaves, goods, wares and merchandizes whatsoever to be rented or found at or within any of the Cities, Towns, places, Rivers situate or being in the Countries, Islands, Places Ports, and Coasts aforementioned, any statute, Law, grant, matter, customs or privilege to the contrary in any wise, notwithstanding ...

Witness the King at Westminster
the seven and twentieth day, 1672,
By the King

An Act for Extending and Improving the Trade to Africa, 1750

(Donnan, Ibid, *Volume I*, p. 473).

Whereas the Trade to and from Africa is very advantageous to Great Britain, and necessary for the supplying the Plantations and Colonies thereunto belonging with a sufficient Number of Negroes at reasonable Rates; and for that Purpose the said Trade ought to be free and open to all his Majesty's Subjects: Therefore be it enacted, and it is hereby enacted by the King's most Excellent Majesty, by and with the Advice and Consent of the Lords Spiritual and Temporal, and Commons, in this present Parliament assembled, and by the Authority of the same, That it shall and may be lawful for all his Majesty's Subjects to trade and traffick to and from any Port or Place in Africa, between the Port of Sallee in South Barbary, and the Cape of Good Hope, when, and at such Times, and in such Manner, and in or with such Quantity of Goods, Wares or Merchandizes, as he or they shall think fit, without any Restraint whatsoever...

Poem

by William Cowper

(Dow, Ibid, 1st page of Chapter V, date unknown).

I own I am shocked at the purchase of slaves,
And fear those who buy them and sell them are knaves;
What I hear of their hardships, their tortures and groans,
Is almost enough to draw pity from stones.
I pity them greatly, but I must be mum,
For how could we do without sugar and rum?

13

The Negroes Complaint

by William Cowper

(From Thomas Clarkson, *The History of the Abolition of the African Slave Trade – Volume 2.* London: Frank Cass & Company Limited, 1968, pp. 188-190, originally published in 1808).

Forced from home and all its pleasures,
    Afric's coast I left forlorn,
To increase a stranger's treasures,
    O'er the raging billows borne;
Men from England bought and sold me,
    Paid my price in paltry gold;
But, though theirs they have inroll'd me,
    Minds are never to be sold ...

By our blood in Afrie wasted,
    Ere our necks received the chain;
By the miseries, which we tasted
    Crossing, in your barks, the main;
By our sufferings, since you brought us
    To the man-degrading mart,
All sustain'd by patience, taught us
    Only by a broken heart:

Deem our nation brutes no longer,
    Till some reason you shall find
Worthier of regard, and stronger,
    Than the colour of our kind.
Slaves of gold! whose sordid dealings
    Tarnish all your boasted powers,
Prove that you have human feelings,
    Ere you proudly question ours.

Account of the Liverpool Slave Trade, 1795

(From Elizabeth Donnan, *Documents Illustrative of the History of the Slave Trade to America – Volume II – The 18th Century*. New York: Octagon Books, Inc., pp. 625, 627, originally published in 1931).

Summary of the aggregate number of ships employed in the Guinea Trade, particularized in the following tables, together with the number of slaves imported in each of the following years and the amount of each.

Years	Slave Ships	Number of Slaves	Sterling Value
1783	85	39,170	L 1,958,500
1784	59	25,320	1,266,000
1785	73	29,490	1,474,500
1786	87	31,690	1,584,500
1787	72	25,520	1,276,000
1788	71	23,200	1,160,000
1789	62	17,631	881,550
1790	89	27,362	1,368,100
1791	101	31,111	1,555,550
1792	133	38,920	1,946,000
1793	46	14,323	716,150
	878	303,737	L 15,186,850

1786

The nett proceeds on thirty-one thousand six hundred and ninety slaves, are		1,282,690
Gross amount of goods exported	864,895	
Freight of 31,690 slaves, etc.	103,488	
Maintenance of 31,690 slaves at ten shillings each	15,845	
	984,228	– 984,228
Gains on the whole [profits]		L 298,462

Letter From William Fitzhugh [Virginia Planter and Merchant] to Mr. Jackson [of Portsmouth, New Hampshire], 1683

(From Elizabeth Donnan, *Documents Illustrative of the History of the Slave Trade to America - Volume IV - The Border Colonies and the Southern Colonies.* New York: Octagon Books, Inc., 1965, p. 57, originally published in 1935).

Mr. Jackson: As to your proposal about the bringing in Negroes next fall, I have this to offer and you may communicate the same to your owners and Employers, that I will deal with them for so many as shall amount to 50,000 lbs of Tob'o [tobacco] and cask [rum] which will be about 20 hhds. [hogsheads, which are large containers] under the condition and at these ages and prices following, to say — to give 3000 lbs Tob'o for every Negro boy or girl, that shall be between the age of Seven and Eleven years old; to give 4000 lbs Tob'o for every youth or girl that shall be between the age of 11 to 15 and to give 5000 lbs Tob'o for every young man or woman that shall be above 15 years of age and not exceed 24, the said Negroes to be delivered at my landing some time in September next, and I to have notice whether they will so agree some time in August next. And I do assure you and so you may acquaint them that upon your delivery and my receipt of the Negroes, according to the ages above mentioned and that they be sound and healthfull at their Delivery , I will give you such sufficient caution for the payment of the Tob'o accordingly by the 20th Decr. then next following as shall be approved of. The ages of the Negroes to be judg'd and determin'd by two or three such honest and reasonable men here as your self shall nominate and appoint...

Letter From Wilkinson and D'Ayrault to Captain David Lindsay, 1754

(From Elizabeth Donnan, *Documents Illustrative of the History of the Slave Trade to America - Volume III - New England and the Middle Colonies*. New York: Octagon Books, Inc., 1965, pp. 148-149, originally published in 1932).

Newport [Rhode Island] June 19th 1754

S'r, you being Master of our Schooner *Siralone* and ready to sail, our orders are that you Imbrace the first oppertunity of wind and weather and Proceed for the Coast of Africa, when plese God you arrive there Dispose of your cargoe on the best terms you Can for Gold, Good Slaves etc when you have finished your trade on the Coast (wch we desire may be with all Convenient Dispatch) Proceed for the Island of Barbadoes where you will find Letters Lodged for you in the hands of Mr. Elias Merivelle with whom Consult in regard to the Sale of your Slaves and if they will fetch Twenty Six pounds Sterling p head round you may dispose of them there and Invest the Produce as pr your orders you will find Lodged there, but If you cannot sell at the above price, Proceed without Loss of time to St. Vincents there dispose of your Slaves. If they will fetch five hundred Livres round in Money, and In case you sell there you may purchase as much Cocoa as you can Carry Under your halfe Deck and proceed to St Eustatia their Load with Molasses and If any opportunity of Fraight ship the remainder of the nett proceeds in Molasses to this Port or to Boston If to Boston Consign it to Messrs Steyh[?] and Wm. Greenleafe. Should you find it will detain you long at St. Eustatia to accomplish this send the Schooner home as soone as Possible after She is Loaded and Come Passinger after you have finished your business but If they will not fetch the above Price Proceed directly for the Island of Jamaica, there you will find orders Lodged for you and dispose of your Slaves on the best terms you can and Invest amount of

the Produce in Good Muscovado sugar or will load you in such
Cask as you can stow with most conveniency and proceed home
with all Possible Dispatch. you are to have four of 104 for your
Coast Commission and five pr Cent for Sales of your Cargoe
in the West Indies and five pr Cent for the Goods you purchase
for return. we desire you will omit no opportunity of Letting
us hear from you we wish you a good Voyage and are your
Loving owners,

Wilkinson and D'Ayrault Jr.

[Reverend] Peter Fontaine to Moses Fontaine, 1757

(Donnan, Ibid, *Volume IV*, pp. 142-143).

March the 30th, 1757

Dear Brother Moses: ...Like Adam we are all apt to shift off
the blame from ourselves and lay it upon others, how justly in
our case you may judge. The negroes are enslaved by the negroes
themselves before they are purchased by the masters of the ships
who bring them here. It is to be sure at our choice whether we
buy them or not, so this then is our crime, folly, or whatever
you will please to call it ... to live in Virginia without slaves
is morally impossible. Before our troubles you could not hire a
servant or slave for love or money, so that unless robust enough
to cut wood, to go to mill, to work at the hoe, etc. you must
starve, or board in some family where they both fleece and half
starve you. There is no set price upon corn, wheat and provisions, so they take advantage of the necessities of strangers,
who are thus obliged to purchase some slaves and land. This
of course draws us all into the original sin and curse of the
country of purchasing slaves, and this is the reason we have
no merchants, traders, or artificers of any sort but what become
planters in a short time.

A common laborer, white or black, if you can be so much favored as to hire one, is a shilling sterling or fifteen pence currency per day; a bungling carpenter two shillings or two shillings and six pence per day; besides diet and lodging. That is, for a lazy fellow to get wood and water, L19, 16.3. current per annum; add to this seven or eight pounds more and you have a slave for life...

Estimates of Blacks as a Percentage of the Population by Colony, 1680-1770

(From Peter Kolchin, *American Slavery 1619-1877*. New York: Hill and Wang, 1993, pp. 240, parts of Table 1 - Appendix).

Colony	1680	1770
North		
New Hampshire	3.7	1.0
Massachusetts	0.4	1.8
Rhode Island	5.8	6.5
Connecticut	0.3	3.1
New York	12.2	11.7
New Jersey	5.9	7.0
Pennsylvania	3.7	2.4
South		
Delaware	5.5	5.2
Maryland	9.0	31.5
Virginia	6.9	42.0
North Carolina	3.9	35.3
South Carolina	16.7	60.5
Georgia	—	45.2
Totals		
North	2.3	4.4
South	5.7	39.7
Thirteen Colonies	4.6	21.4

The Triangular Trade

Although direct trade routes from one region to another were frequent in colonial commerce, the triangular trade route was characteristic of the Atlantic slave trade.

There were two main patterns of triangular trade. The first was a voyage from England to Africa, on to the West Indies, and then back to England. For example, a slave ship would leave the English port of Liverpool with a cargo of manufactured goods, then proceed to West Africa where these items were exchanged for slaves. The slaves were transported to the West Indies and sold, and the profits were used to purchase a cargo of sugar (or other produce) which was brought back to Liverpool.

The second pattern of triangular trade originated in New England. Slave ships sailed to West Africa with a cargo of rum and they exchanged the rum for slaves. Then they headed on to the slave markets of the West Indies where the slaves were sold. The profits of the sale were used to purchase cargoes of molasses, which were brought back to New England and distilled into rum.

Although the corners of the triangle often varied, slaves, rum, sugar, molasses, tobacco, and other crops played vital roles in the trade.

The following excerpts focus on each leg of the triangular trade route, giving the reader an authentic picture of the realities of the African slave trade.

First Leg – Voyage to Africa

A typical slave ship leaving New England for Africa in the 18th century carried a cargo mainly of rum and small amounts of tobacco, muskets, soap, flour, and other items. A slaver out of Liverpool generally carried textiles, metalware, firearms and gunpowder, wool and cotton cloth, fine linens of all colors and patterns, knives, beads, jewelry, brandy, rum, and other goods.

The destination for both vessels was typically the Guinea slave coast of West Africa, between the Senegal and Congo Rivers. Here regions called Loango, Gambia, the Gold Coast, Goree, Whydah, Calibar, Bonny, and Dahomey provided slave labor to the rest of the world for the nearly four hundred years of the Atlantic slave trade.

Once in West Africa, slaves could be obtained in two ways. The Europeans built forts, also called slave factories, along the coast early in the trade. Here, a factor, who was a representative of a particular country or company, would negotiate with the local African kings and slave traders to supply slaves at an agreed upon price. The slaves would be kept within the forts until enough were assembled to load onto the slave ships.

Frequently, ships anchored off the coast or at the mouth of a river. The ship's captain or representative negotiated directly with local African kings and black slave traders to purchase a cargo of slaves. It often took weeks to months to accumulate a full cargo. While negotiations took place, crew members built a house or enclosed pen (called a barracoon) on the deck of their vessels. These were used to collect and guard newly purchased slaves until the ships were ready to set sail.

The following excerpts focus on the slavery system in Africa and the methods used to obtain slaves for the Atlantic trade.

21

The Slave Ship

by Henrich Heine

(From James A. Rawley, *The Transatlantic Slave Trade*, New York: W.W. Norton & Company, 1981, p. 303).

Six hundred niggers I bought dirt-cheap
  Where the Senegal river is flowing;
Their flesh is firm, and their sinews tough
  As the finest iron going.

I got them by barter, and gave in exchange
  Glass beads, steel goods, and some brandy;
I shall make at least eight hundred per cent
  With but half of them living and handy.

John Barbot's Description of Guinea

(Donnan, Ibid, *Volume II*, pp. 284, 287,289, 292-294, 297, first published by Barbot in 1732).

Slaves. Those sold by the Blacks are for the most part prisoners of war, taken either in fight, or pursuit, or in the incursions they make into their enemies territories; others stolen away by their own countrymen...The kings are so absolute, that upon any slight pretence of offences committed by their subjects, they order them to be sold for slaves, without regard to rank, or possession... In times of dearth and famine, abundance of those people will sell themselves, for a maintenance, and to prevent starving...some slaves are also brought to these Blacks, from very remote inland countries, by way of trade, and sold for things of very inconsiderable value... This country [Acra] is continually in war with some of the neighbouring nations, which are very populous, and from whom they take very many prisoners, most of whom, they sell... At other times slaves are so scarce there, that in 1682, I could get but eight from one end of the coast to the other not only becase we were a great number of trading ships on the coast at the same time, but by reason the natives were every where at peace...

Of the Slave Coast... The rate in trade is generally adjusted with the king, and none permitted to buy or sell till that is proclaimed; whereby he reserves to himself the preference in all dealings, he for the most part having the greatest number of slaves, which are sold at a set price, the women a fourth or a fifth cheaper than the men. This done, and the king's customs paid...the factor has full liberty to trade... As the slaves come down...from the inland country, they are put into a booth, or prison, built for that purpose, near the beach, all of them together; and when the Europeans are to receive them, they are brought out into a large plain, where the surgeons examine every part of every one of them... Such as are allowed good and sound, are set on one side, and the others by themselves; which slaves so rejected are there called Mackrons, being above thirty five years of age, or defective in their limbs, eyes or teeth; or grown grey, or that have the venereal disease, or any other im-perfection. Those being so set aside, each of the others, which have passed as good, is marked on the breast, with a red-hot iron, imprinting the mark of the French, English, or Dutch companies, that so each nation may distinguish their own, and to prevent their being chang'd by the natives for worse, as they are apt enough to do. In this particular, care is taken that the women, as tenderest, be not burnt too hard.

The branded slaves, after this, are returned to their former booth, where the factor is to subsist them at his own charge, which amounts to about two-pence a day for each of them, with bread and water, which is all their allowance. There they continue sometimes ten or fifteen days, till the sea is still enough to send them aboard...the slaves are carried off by parcels, in bar-canoes,

23

and put aboard the ships in the road. Before they enter the canoes, or come out of the booth, their former Black masters strip them of every rag they have, without distinction of men or women; to supply which, in orderly ships, each of them as they come aboard is allowed a piece of canvas, to wrap around their waist, which is very acceptable to those poor wretches... The factor...having finished his sale, is to present the king again with two muskets, twenty five pounds of powder, and the value of nine slaves in other goods, as an acknowledgement to that prince for his favour in granting him the permission to trade in his dominions...

Sins of the Fathers

by James Pope-Hennessy

(From James Pope-Hennessy, *Sins of the Fathers*, New York: Alfred A. Knopf, 1968, pp. 202-203, 880).

...When slaves were hard to come by, certain captains would organize their own regular white raiding parties on shore. Boats from a number of ships would put off together, 'to take whomever we could catch,' as one member of such an expedition put it. They would steal into a native town or village, snatch up any human being they saw and throw their victims, bound and their mouths stuffed...into the bottoms of the boat which would be lying...in the river. On these adventures the sailors all went armed...

This piecemeal ravaging of the coast is symptomatic of the lengths to which, in lean times, eighteenth-century slavers would go to assemble their cargoes; but for real bulk-buying they always depended on encouraging local potentates to embark on raids which they dignified by the title 'war with the neighbours.' These 'wars' were indeed nothing more than pillaging expeditions for human loot...

The status of domestic slaves in Africa differed...from area to area and from tribe to tribe. The most usual method of enslavement was as payment for a bad debt—when a man would pledge himself and his family indefinitely in a form of serfdom to his creditor. Further reasons for enslavement were adultery, theft and certain other crimes. West African slavery was a vital part of a general social and political structure... The different African kingdoms had their own rules for the protection of their slaves. In Benin, for instance, no male Bini could be sold for export. Here, as almost universally elsewhere along the coast, the European slave-market was supplied by prisoners taken in war, by enslaved criminals or by Africans captured or kidnapped from other tribes...

Thomas Clarkson's Efficiency of Regulation of the Slave Trade

(The testimony of witnesses as reported by Clarkson, from Donnan, Ibid, *Volume II*, p. 572)

...I had two opportunities of seeing how slaves were procured in the River of Old Calabar. I resided with the king of New Town for four months, and he allowed me to go up the river with him to trade for slaves. I went with him twice within that time. In the first expedition, there was a fleet consisting of from ten to twelve canoes, which were properly manned and armed. With this fleet we set out to trade. In the day time we called at the villages as we passed, and purchased our slaves fairly; but in the night we made several excursions on the banks of the river. The canoes were usually left with an armed force: the rest, when landed, broke into the villages, and, rushing into the huts of the inhabitants, seized men, women, and children...We obtained about fifty negroes in this manner, in our first expedition.

In our second, the same practices were in force; for we traded fairly by day, and became robbers in the night...

Testimony of William James, Sea Captain
Bristol, England

(Donnan, Ibid, *Volume II*, p. 398).

...The Black Traders of Bonny and Calabar, who are very expert at reckoning and talking the different Languages of their own Country and those of the Europeans, come down about once a Fortnight with Slaves; Thursday or Friday is generally their Trading Day. Twenty or Thirty Canoes, sometimes more and sometimes less, come down at a Time. In each Canoe may be Twenty or Thirty Slaves. The Arms of some of them are tied behind their Backs with Twigs, Canes, Grass Rope, or other Ligaments of the Country; and if they happen to be stronger than common, they are pinioned above the Knee also. In this Situation they are thrown into the Bottom of the Canoe, where they lie in great Pain, and often almost covered with Water. On their landing, they are taken to the Traders Houses, where they are oiled, fed, and made up for Sale...

✖ ✖ ✖ ✖

Each region in Africa had a special type of currency that was used to price slaves and other goods. In Guinea, bars of iron were used in trade. According to Dr. T. Winterbottom in *An Account of the Native Africans in Sierra Leone*, "From Senegal to Cape Mesurado on the Windward Coast...the medium of computation is termed a bar... The bar...is like one pound sterling, merely nominal, but even less precise in its value, and subject to great irregularities. Moreover the quantity of an article contained in a bar differs, not only on various parts of the coast, but often in neighboring rivers. A gun valued at twenty shillings," explained Winterbottom, "is sold for six bars; but the same number of bars of tobacco will only be equal in value to four or five shillings...A piece of cloth which in one place passes for six bars, passes in others for eight, and in others for ten..."

In Whydah and other areas along the Slave Coast, small milk-white sea shells called "cowries" were the currency of choice. 40 cowries, threaded on a string, were called toques. At one time, 100 toques (or 4000 cowries) were equal in value to either one pound sterling (a pound of English silver pennies), one English gold sovereign, or one-quarter ounce of gold dust. Trade was conducted in other areas of Africa by "goods" and "pieces."

The Trade in Loango
by Abbe Proyart

(Donnan, Ibid, *Volume II*, pp. 549-551).

...Though the different kingdoms of which we are speaking be not far distant from each other; the manner of valuing goods and turning slaves to account is not uniform among them...in the kingdoms of Kakongo and n'Goio, they reckon by goods; and in Loango by pieces; what they call goods, is a piece of cotton or Indian cloth ten or fourteen ells long. [An ell, which varies from country to country, is a measure of length from 27 to 45 inches]. The negroes before striking a bargain go and mark off at the captain's store...the pieces of stuffs they choose to take; and he who has sold four slaves at fifteen goods a head, goes to receive sixty pieces of the stuffs marked off. In the kingdoms where they buy by goods it is customary to give fore each slave what is called 'the over and above,' which commonly consists of three or four guns and as many swords; fifteen pots of brandy, fifteen pounds of gunpowder, and some dozens of knives. If these articles be not always given them, others are substituted as an equivalent.

27

At Loango they reckon by pieces, and every sort of goods is entered in a line of the account with the stuffs to form the piece; thus, when they say a slave costs thirty pieces, it does not mean he costs thirty pieces of stuffs, but thirty times the ideal value which they think fit to fix on, and call a piece; so that a single piece of stuff is sometimes estimated at two or three pieces, as sometimes several objects must form a single piece...

I have paid at Ma-nboukou, for the slave Makviota, twenty-two years of age, whom he has sold me at thirty pieces,

An indienne of fourteen ells valued at
    two and a half pieces...2 1/2

Two guineas (they are cotton cloths dyed deep blue)
    each valued at two and a half pieces......................5

A chaffelat (white grape), and a bajutapeau (hog's
    cheek), fourteen ells each (they are cotton cloths)
    estimated at four pieces.....................................4

A neganopeau of 14 ells and a great nicane of
    9 1/2 ells (other cotton cloths), estimated at
    three and a half pieces.....................................3 1/2

A piece of handkerchiefs of 9 ells, estimated at
    a piece and a half..1 1/2

A rod (about an ell and a quarter of thick woolen stuff)
    estimated at a piece..1

A girdle of red cloth (an ell long by a foot broad)
    estimated at a piece..1

Two common guns, valued at two pieces...................2

Two barrels of gunpowder (about 5 lbs. each)
    valued at two pieces...2

Two bags of leaden musket balls, (weight 3 lbs. each)
    valued at half a piece......................................0 1/2

Two swords, valued at each a quarter of a piece...........0 1/2

Two dozens of common sheath knives, estimated at
    half a piece 0 1/2

Two bars of iron (weight both together 20 lb.)
    valued at a piece.. 1

Five pots of Dutch ware, valued at half a piece 0 1/2

Four barrels of brandy, each containing five pots,
    valued at four pieces 4

Ten strings of bugles (glass beads, of which chaplets
    [necklaces] are made) valued at half a piece............. 0 1/2

                                    Total .... 30 pieces

I have paid moreover to the broker for his trouble
    the value of six pieces in guns, powder, swords,
    and brandy .... 6 pieces
                                                    36 pieces

Besides the pieces determined on for each slave, the captain
must also, ere the bargain be closed, make a present to...the
brokers who have served him best, and whom he is very glad
to attach to himself: these presents are made in coral, services
of plate, carpets, and other moveables, more or less precious...

The Middle Passage

The second leg of the triangular trade route was called the "middle passage." This was the ocean crossing from the African coast to the slave markets of the West Indies.

The ships were packed from bow to stern with men, women, and children, who were forced to live in unclean conditions where disease flourished. Slaves were allowed only the minimum of food and water. They were exposed daily to the brutalities of the crewmen and captain and often endured long, slow voyages.

Mortality rates for slaves during the middle passage were extraordinarily high. Philip D. Curtin in *The Atlantic Slave Trade* estimated the death rate was from thirteen percent to thirty-three percent depending on the length of the voyage. The longer the time at sea, the more likely the ship would run short of food and water, causing a greater loss of slaves due to disease and dehydration.

The mortality rate for crew members was nearly as high as the slaves on certain voyages. Diseases such as smallpox, measles, dysentery, malaria, hookworm, and a deadly eye infection called ophthalmia spread quickly on slave ships.

Although some voyages were made without the loss of a single slave, epidemics could wipe out hundreds at a time. One English vessel, the Hero, lost 360 slaves to smallpox.

Some ships were packed with slaves as tightly as possible, giving them little room to move around. This allowed for larger slave cargoes, but loss of life on these voyages was often greater than on looser-packed ships with smaller cargoes. Slave merchants argued that although more slaves died during the middle passage on tighter-packed ships, the larger cargoes resulted in more slaves surviving, and thus greater profits overall.

The crowded and filthy conditions in the slave quarters as well as the heat and stench caused many of the Africans to go mad and attempt suicide by jumping overboard. Some became so depressed and upset about being forced to leave their homeland that they had no wish to live and starved themselves to death. Crewmen prevented suicides whenever they could and force fed the slaves, since their profits were dependent upon getting as many as possible to the West Indies alive.

Slaves were killed during the middle passage for various reasons. Some slaves were thrown overboard as examples to others to prevent mutinies or possible slave revolts. On particularly long trips, when provisions were low and disease was rampant, some captains threw sick slaves overboard in order to collect on their insurance policy.

Insurance on slave ships covered death by drowning but not by starvation or disease. In one famous case, the *Zong*, out of Liverpool, carried 440 slaves to Jamaica from the African Coast. With an outbreak of dysentary on board and a shortage of food and water, Captain Luke Collingwood ordered 132 weak and sick Africans thrown overboard so the ship owners could collect the insurance money.

When the owners tried to claim the money, the insurance company refused to pay and the case went to court in England. The judges ruled for the owners because the law treated slaves as merchandise.

Parliament first regulated the slave trade in 1788, requiring each ship to have a certified surgeon (or doctor) on board and keep a journal of deaths during the voyage. The law provided a bonus to the doctor and the ship's captain if no more than three slaves per hundred (three percent) died during the middle passage.

The law also limited the number of slaves per ship's ton, in an effort to reduce mortality. Five slaves were allowed for every three tons (up to 201 tons), and one slave for each additional ton.

Insurance was outlawed on slave cargoes with the exceptions of "perils of the sea" and fire.

In 1799, the law was extended even further, requiring certain minimum space standards for each slave carried. "Every man slave [was allowed] six feet by one foot four inches for room, every woman five feet ten by one foot four, every boy five feet by one foot two and every girl four feet six by one foot." (Donnan, *Volume II*, p. 592, and Clarkson, p. 113). Even with the new law in effect, the bodies of slaves were still packed together in most slave ships.

The following excerpts focus on the middle passage and include several first-person accounts of the condition and treatment of slaves, during the oftentimes long and difficult voyage.

Sins of the Fathers
by James Pope-Hennessy

(Pope-Hennessy, Ibid, p. 279).

...the portrait of a slave ship lying off the Isles de Los on the Windward Coast of Guinea in the summer-time of the year 1773.

This description of *The African*, commanded by a Captain Wilding, is given in the journal of the English botanist, Henry Smeathman, who was spending four years on the Banana Islands collecting specimens of plants for English amateurs.

'Alas!' (he writes) 'what a scene of misery and distress is a full slaved ship in the rains.' He found the clank of fetters, the groans and the stench almost insupportable. Two officers lay delirious in the cabin. Every day two or three slaves dying of the flux [dysentery], measles or worms, were dropped overboard to the sharks. The sound of the armourer riveting irons on the new arrivals mingled with that of dragging chains, and with the thudding of pestles as the women slaves pounded the rice in mortars. There was the ship's doctor dressing slaves' sores and

ulcers, and cramming their mouths with medicines while a sea-
man stood over the patients with a cat-o'-nine-tails [a whip] to
force them to swallow the draught. Casks, boxes and bales were
being hauled on board with creaking tackles, and the carpenter
and cooper were hammering away, while others filed and cleaned
arms. The barber was shaving slaves' heads, holding his victims
by the nose. Goods were being stored everywhere, and the mates
would watch over the slaves eating their rice from the little tubs
called 'crews' round which six or eight Negroes squatted, using
their fingers... Negroes were using the open latrine near which
slave women were washing dirty linen and wiping crockery...

Adventures of an African Slaver

by Theophilus Conneau

(From Malcolm Cowley, Editor. *Adventures of An African Slaver*. New York:
Albert and Charles Boni Publishers, 1928, pp. 107-108).

...An African factor of fair repute is ever careful to select
his human cargo with consummate prudence, so as not only to
supply his employers with athletic labourers, but to avoid any
taint of disease that may affect the slaves in their transit... Two
days before embarkation, the head of every male and female is
neatly shaved; and, if the cargo belongs to several owners, each
man's brand is impressed on the body of his respective negro.
This operation is performed with pieces of silver wire, or small
irons fashioned into the merchant's initials, heated just hot
enough to blister without burning the skin. When the entire
cargo is the venture of but one proprietor, the branding is
always dispensed with.

On the apponted day, the barracoon or slave-pen is made joy-
ous by the abundant 'feed' which signalises the negro's last hours
in his native country. The feast over, they are taken alongside the
vessel in canoes...

Observations of Captain Thomas Phillips
of the Hannibal

(From Daniel P. Mannix, *Black Cargoes*. New York: Viking Press, 1961, p. 48).

The negroes are so wilful and loth to leave their own country, that they have often leap'd out of the canoos, boat and ship, into the sea, and kept under water till they were drowned, to avoid being taken up and saved by our boats, which pursued them; they having a more dreadful apprehension of Barbadoes than we can have of hell...We have likewise seen divers of them eaten by the sharks, of which a prodigious number kept about the ships in this place, and I have been told will follow her hence to Barbadoes, for the dead negroes that are thrown overboard in the passage...

Thoughts Upon the Atlantic Slave Trade
by Reverend John Newton

(Mannix, Ibid, p. 106).

The cargo of a vessel of a hundred tons or a little more is calculated to purchase from 220 to 250 slaves. Their lodging rooms below the deck which are three (for the men, the boys and the women) besides a place for the sick, are sometimes more than five feet high and sometimes less; and this height is divided toward the middle for the slaves lie in two rows, one above the other, on each side of the ship, close to each other like books upon a shelf. I have known them so close that the shelf would not easily contain one more.

The poor creatures, thus cramped, are likewise in irons for the most part which makes it difficult for them to turn or move or attempt to rise or to lie down without hurting themselves or each other. Every morning, perhaps, more instances than one are found of the living and the dead fastened together.

A Slaver's Log Book or 20 Years Residence in Africa

by Captain Theophilus Conneau

(From Theophilus Conneau, *A Slaver's Log Book or 20 Years Residence in Africa.* Englewood Cliffs, New Jersey: Prentice-Hall, Inc., 1976, pp. 82-84, 192-195, originally published in 1854).

...At mealtime...[the slaves]... are distributed ten to a mess ...a bucket full of salt water is given to each mess...[and] they are made to wash their hands. Then a kid [wooden tub] is placed before them full of either rice, farina, yams or beans, according to what country they belong, as Negroes from the south do not eat the same food as those from the north. At a signal given they all dip their hands and in rotation take out a handful, a sailor watching their movements and the punctuality of the regular turn.

It is the sailor's duty to report when any one of the slaves refuses to eat, and if...it is found that stubbornness is the cause of a voluntary abstinence (Negroes often starve themselves to death), the cat is applied till a cure is effected...

The feeding over, another bucket of water is given for a second washing, and everyone is then allowed to retire in single file manner to their favorite plank about decks or below. This duty of feeding takes place twice a day, at 10 in the morning and at 4 in the afternoon. Water is also given three times a day, a half pint each time... Thrice a week their mouth is washed with vinegar, and nearly every morning a dram of spirits is given them, both used as preservative against scurvy...

Corporal chastisement is only inflicted by order of the officers, and then the culprit is made to understand why he is chastised. Once a week the barber goes the round with his attendants and scrapes without the assistance of soap their wiry chins, free of expense. The fingernails are also cropped every shaving day...

The sick are separated as soon as discovered. The whole of the forecastle is appropriated exclusively for the sick slave....

35

The Boatswain's duty is to keep the ship clean, and this is attended with the greatest scrupulosity. Every morning at daylight all the filth of the night is removed and the tubs scrubbed with chloride of lime...

At sundown the Second Mate and Boatswain descend, cat in hand, and stow the Negroes for the night. Those on the starboard side face forward and in one another's lap, ...called spoon fashion. On the port side they are stowed with face aft; this position is considered preferable for the free pulsation of the heart. The tallest are selected for the greatest breadth of the vessel, while the short size and youngsters are stowed in the forepart of the ship. Great precaution is also taken to place those such as may have sores or boils on the side most convenient... Tubs are also distributed on the sleeping deck and so placed that both sides can have access. (The sick are never placed below.)

The lower deck once full, the rest are stowed on the deck, which is prepared with loose boards to keep the water from under them; they are then covered in fair weather with spare sails and with tarpaulins in rainy nights. In this manner they are made to remain all night, if possible. This discipline of stowing them is of the greatest importance on board slavers...

Every slaver's hatches and bulkheads are grated, and additional small hatches are cut about the decks for the greater circulation of air; wind sails and every communication with the hold are constantly kept up, unless in a chase, when every comfort is sacrificed for the safety of the vessel. When in light winds or calms and the wind sails are useless, the gratings are taken off and a portion of the slaves are allowed to lay on the deck, under guard of the whole crew which are ever armed on such occasion.

For the security and safekeeping of the slaves on board... chains, leg irons, handcuffs, and strong houses are used. I would remark that this also is one of the forcible necessities resorted to for the preservation of order, and as recourse against the dangerous consequences of this traffic. Irons and handcuffs are used on board with as much frugality as possible. Slaves are generally brought on board chained ten in a gang... but as these chains are very inconvenient on board, they are taken off immediately, and leg irons put on which secures them two by two, the right of the one fastened to the left of the other. They consist of a bolt a foot long with two shackles, and are only put on to full grown men. Women and boys are let loose on their arrival on board...

We had been off Cape Good Hope for several days, buffeting a continuation of contrary gales, when after a long night of watching and toil I was made aware that several of our slaves were discovered with the smallpox...

During the gale which had lasted nine days, our slaves had forcibly been neglected. Not once had they been allowed to visit the decks. The gratings had been partly covered during the gale to keep the slave deck dry from the seas and rains. The wind sails could not be kept up, and ventilation had circulated but slightly during the time.

At the first announcement that a slave had been found dead by the morning inspector, the Officer of the Watch had inspected the body, and its appearance denoted the well-known token of smallpox. It was kept silent from the slaves and the body thrown silently over the board. After breakfast I visited the slave deck with lanterns, and to my great dismay, nine of the slaves were found affected with the dreadful disease...

The sick were immediately placed in the hospital (the forecastle) and every precaution taken that only those of our crew that had been vaccinated should attend them. The lower deck was fumigated, and chloride of lime sprinkled at every habitable part of the ship, and nothing was left undone that would stop the progress of the epidemic.

The abated gale lasted two days longer, and the number of the sick had accumulated to 30. The dreadful scourge was progressing with giant strides, the hospital could not contain one more, and

12 of my men had caught the distemper. Before night of this day, the number of deaths amounted to 15.

...Dead man after dead man went over the board as they expired, and the day that we conveniently opened all the gratings, our consternation rose to its climax. Nearly all our slaves had the distemper. Twelve of the stoutest were singled out to attend to the dragging out of the dead from the sick, and although they were constantly fed with rum to brutalize them in the disgusting job, still we were forced to have recourse to such of our crew as were not affected, who with tarred mittens picked up the still warm bodies to remove them to the porthole...

Our misfortune ended only when 497 living skeletons were left out of eight hundred prime Negroes shipped a few weeks before in good health.

An Account of the Slave Trade

by Dr. Alexander Falconbridge

(first published in London, 1788, from Pope-Hennessy, Ibid, p. 102).

Some wet and blowing weather having occasioned the portholes to be shut, and the grating to be covered, fluxes and fevers among the negroes ensued. While they were in this situation, my profession requiring it, I frequently went down among them, till at length their apartments became so extremely hot as to be only sufferable for a very short time. But the excessive heat was not the only thing that rendered their situation intolerable. The deck, that is the floor of their rooms, was so covered with the blood and mucous which had proceeded from them in consequence of the flux, that it resembled a slaughter-house. It is not in the power of the human imagination to picture to itself a situation more dreadful or disgusting. Numbers of the slaves having fainted, they were carried up on deck, where several of them died and the rest were, with great difficulty, restored...

Journal of Richard Drake

(Pope-Hennessy, Ibid, p. 4).

I am growing sicker every day of this business of buying and selling human beings for beasts of burden... On the eighth day [out at sea] I took my round of the half deck, holding a camphor bag in my teeth; for the stench was hideous. The sick and dying were chained together. I saw pregnant women give birth to babies whilst chained to corpses, which our drunken overseers had not removed. The blacks were literally jammed between decks as if in a coffin, and a coffin that dreadful hold became to nearly one half of our cargo before we reached Bahia.

Diary of J.B. Romaigne

(Twelve-year-old passenger who sailed on slaver Le Rodeur in 1819 from France to Africa to the West Indies.)

(From "Introduction" by Ernest Pentecost in Dow, pp. xxviii - xxxv).

III

...Today, one of the blacks whom they were forcing into the hold, suddenly knocked down a sailor and attempted to leap overboard. He was caught, however, by the leg by another of the crew, and the sailor, rising up in a passion, hamstrung him with a cutlass. The Captain, seeing this, knocked the butcher flat upon the deck with a handspike. 'I will teach you to keep your temper,' said he, with an oath. 'He was the best slave in the lot.' I ran to the main chains and looked over; for they had dropped the black into the sea when they saw that he was useless. He continued to swim, even after he had sunk under water, for I saw the red track extending shoreward; but by and by, it stopped, widened, faded, and I saw it no more.

IV

...The Captain...walks the deck, rubbing his hands and humming a tune. He says he has six dozen slaves on board, men, women and children, and all in prime marketable condition. I have not seen them, however, since we set sail. Their cries are so terrible that I do not like to go and look down into the hold. At first, I could not close my eyes; the sound froze my very blood...

V

Today, word was brought to the Captain, while we were at breakfast, that two of the slaves were dead, suffocated, as was supposed, by the closeness of the hold; and he immediately ordered the rest should be brought up, gang by gang, to the forecastle, to give them air. I ran up on deck to see them...

However, they had no sooner reached the ship's side, than first one, then another, then a third, sprang up on the gunwale, and darted into the sea, before the astonished sailors could tell what they were about. Many more made the attempt, but without success; they were all knocked flat to the deck, and the crew kept watch over them with handspikes and cutlasses till the Captain's pleasure should be known with regard to the revolt.

The negroes, in the meantime, who had got off, continued dancing about among the waves, yelling with all their might, what seemed to me a song of triumph, in the burden of which they were joined by some of their companions on deck. Our ship speedily left the ignorant creatures behind; their voices came fainter and fainter upon the wind; the black head, first of one, then of another, disappeared; and then the sea was without a spot; and the air without a sound.

When the Captain came up on deck, having finished his breakfast, and was told of the revolt, his face grew pale, and he gnashed his teeth. 'We must make an example,' said he, 'or our labour will be lost.' He then ordered the whole of the slaves in the ship

to be tied together in gangs and placed upon the forecastle, and
having selected six, who were known to have joined in the chorus
of the revolters and might thus be considered as the ringleaders,
he caused three of them to be shot, and the other three hanged,
before the eyes of their comrades.

VII

The negroes, ever since the revolt, were confined closely to the
lower hold and this brought on a disease called ophthalmia, which
produced blindness. The sailors, who sling down the provisions
from the upper hold, report that the disease is spreading fright-
fully... The patient is at first blind; but some escape, eventually,
with the loss of one eye or a mere dimness of vision. The result
of the conversation was, that the infected slaves were to be transferred to the upper hold and attended by the surgeon the same as
if they were white men.

VIII

All of the slaves and some of the crew are blind. The Captain,
the surgeon, and the mate are blind. There is hardly enough men
left, out of our twenty-two, to work the ship. The Captain pre-
serves what order he can and the surgeon still attempts to do his
duty, but our situation is frightful.

IX

All the crew are now blind but one man. The rest work under
his orders like unconscious machines...My own eyes begin to be
affected; in a little while, I shall see nothing but death...

X

Mother, your son was blind for ten days, although now so
well as to be able to write. I can tell you hardly anything of our
history during that period...

XI

The man who preserved his sight the longest, recovered the soonest; and to his exertions alone...we are now within a few leagues of Guadaloupe, this twenty-first day of June, 1819. I am myself almost well. The surgeon and eleven more are irrecoverably blind; the Captain has lost one eye; four others have met with the same calamity; and five are able to see, though dimly, with both. Among the slaves, thirty-nine are completely blind and the rest blind of one eye or their sight otherwise injured.

This morning the Captain called all hands on deck, negroes and all. The shores of Guadaloupe were in sight. I thought he was going to return God thanks publicly for our miraculous escape.

'Are you quite certain,' said the mate, 'that the cargo is insured?'

'I am,' said the Captain. 'Every slave that is lost must be made good by the underwriters. Besides, would you have me turn my ship into a hospital for the support of blind negroes? They have cost us enough already. Do your duty.'

The mate picked out thirty-nine negroes who were completely blind, and, with the assistance of the rest of the crew, tied a piece of ballast to the legs of each. The miserable wretches were then thrown into the sea.

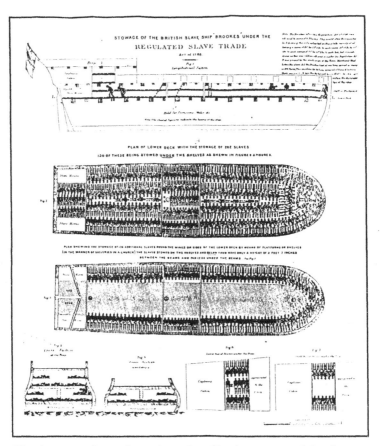

The diagram above shows how, by allowing a space 6 feet long by 1 foot 4 inches wide to each man, 454 slaves could be transported in the British slave ship Brookes.

The West Indies and Home

Shortly before arriving in the West Indies, the captain and crew of the slave ship cleaned, oiled, and fattened up the cargo with extra rations in preparation for the sale. The marketing of the slaves was often supervised by the ship owner's agents or by the captain himself.

Sometimes the entire shipload of Africans were unable to be sold if the quality of the slaves was poor, or the market was weak and the demand low. If this occurred, the captain would proceed from port to port, for weeks or even months, attempting to sell his remaining slaves.

For the most part, the slaves were happy to have reached their destination at last and be off the ship and on dry land. They had no idea of the life of hard labor that lay ahead of them in the sugar plantations of the West Indies (or the tobacco, rice, indigo, and cotton plantations of North America, if that was their destination).

Many of the American colonies received slave shipments directly from the West Indies or, in a variation of the triangular trade, the slaves were carried from Africa to ports in Virginia or South Carolina and sold before the ships returned home.

Once their cargo was disposed of, the captain supervised the cleaning of the ship, making it ready to carry sugar, molasses, tobacco, or other goods and produce, back to their home ports in Europe or America. The third side of the triangle was complete, and the cycle would begin again.

Sins of the Fathers

by James Pope-Hennessy

(Pope-Hennessy, Ibid, p. 104-105).

When a ship laden with slaves dropped anchor off a West Indian port, excitement would prevail on board...The long and noisome voyage was over...the second, and worst, lap of the Triangular Trade was completed once again...

In their merciful ignorance, the slaves, too, rejoiced. Their irons were struck off, they were given fattening foods, and rubbed with oil until their black skins shone in the clear, cool dawn. Suddenly they felt a sense of freedom, curiosity and joy...

On shore, the arrival of a well-stocked Guineaman gave a thrill of anticipatory satisfaction to two mainly unattractive groups — firstly to the ships' agents and the slave-auctioneers, secondly to the owners of plantations...

...[Planters] concluded that to wear slaves out and buy a fresh stock was cheapest in the long run...

Thoughts Upon the Atlantic Slave Trade

by Reverend John Newton

(Pope-Hennessy, Ibid, p. 104).

...The condition of the unhappy slaves is in a continual progress from bad to worse...perhaps they would wish to spend the remainder of their days on ship-board, could they know beforehand the nature of the servitude which awaits them on shore; and that the dreadful hardships and sufferings they have already endured would, to the most of them, only terminate in excessive toil, hunger and the excruciating tortures of the cart-whip, inflicted at the caprice of an unfeeling overseer, proud of the power allowed him of punishing whom, and when, and how he pleases.

An Account of the Slave Trade
by Alexander Falconbridge

(Dow, Ibid, pp. 151-153, first published in 1788).

...When the ships arrive in the West Indies the slaves are disposed of by different methods. Sometimes the mode of disposal is that of selling them by what is termed a scramble and a day is soon fixed for that purpose. But previously the sick or refuse slaves, of which there are frequently many, are usually taken on shore and sold at a tavern, by...public auction...at so low a price as five or six dollars a head...Sometimes the captains march their slaves through the town at which they intend to dispose of them and then place them in rows where they are examined and purchased.

The mode of selling them by scramble is most common. Here, all the negroes scrambled for bear an equal price; which is agreed upon between the captains and the purchasers before the sale begins. On a day appointed, the negroes are landed and placed altogether in a large yard belonging to the merchants to whom the ship is consigned. As soon as the hour agreed on arrives, the doors of the yard are suddenly thrown open and in rushes a considerable number of purchasers, with all the ferocity of brutes. Some instantly seize such of the negroes as they can conveniently lay hold of with their hands. Others, being prepared with several handkerchiefs tied together, encircle with these as many as they are able; while others, by means of a rope, effect the same purpose. It is scarcely possible to describe the confusion of which this mode of selling is productive...The poor astonished negroes are so much terrified by these proceedings, that several of them, on one occasion, climbed over the walls of the courtyard and ran wild about the town but were soon hunted down and retaken...

One of the first narratives written in the late 1700s by Olaudah Equiano gives a first-hand account from a former slave's point of view. Equiano was captured in Benin in Eastern Nigeria at the age of eleven in 1756 and taken to Barbados to be sold. The following excerpt describes the slave market.

An Account of Being Sold

by Olaudah Equiano (renamed Gustaves Vassa)

(from Olaudah Equiano or (renamed Gustaves Vassa), *The Interesting Narrative of the Life of Olaudah Equiano or Gustaves Vassa, The African.* New York: 1791).

[I was] conducted immediately to the merchant's yard, where we were all pent up together like so many sheep in a fold...

I remember...there were several brothers, who in the sale were sold in different lots...

Over thirty years later, when Equiano's journal was published, he cried out in anguish at this cruel practice:

O, ye nominal Christians! might not an African ask you, learned you this from your God, who says unto you, Do unto all men as you would men should do unto you? Is it not enough that we are torn from our country and friends, to toil for your luxury and lust of gain? ... Are the dearest friends and relations, now rendered more dear by their separation from their kindred, still to be parted from each other, and thus prevented from cheering the gloom of slavery with the small comfort of being together and mingling their sufferings and sorrows?

Eventually, Equiano bought his freedom and moved to London. He did make several journies to the Caribbean and to America during his lifetime and was a noted abolititionist until his death in 1797.

Abolition and the Illegal Trade

Whether it was caused by developing industrialization or new moral values, the slave trade was legally abolished in England in 1807 and in the United States in 1808. Other nations followed in prohibiting the African trade in the first half of the 19th century.

However, the great demand for slave labor continued — in the sugar plantations of Cuba, the cotton plantations of the American south, and in the copper mines and coffee, tobacco, and sugar plantations of Brazil.

Despite the risks of being caught by patrolling English war ships, which released the slaves, confiscated the vessel, and often imprisoned the captain, the illegal trade went on, and in fact, flourished. This occurred mainly because of the enormous profits that could be made by successful voyages. A typical field slave, worth $500 before the trade was abolished, was worth three to four times that amount afterwards.

One effect of the illegal trade was that faster slave ships were built which had a better chance of outrunning the English cruisers. The increased risk of being caught caused captains to crowd more slaves on board in less space, resulting in a higher mortality rate, harsher treatment and smaller rations for the black cargoes they carried.

No vessel could be seized by the British as a slave ship unless Africans were actually found on board as evidence. Sometimes cruel captains avoided capture by eliminating the evidence. A story was told about a captain named Homans from the slaver Brillante who was once surrounded by four British vessels just as night fell.

Homans brought his 600 slaves on deck and tied them to the large anchor chain that was stretched around the outside of the ship. When British boats were heard approaching the Brillante, Homans ordered the anchor dropped into the sea, dragging the 600 slaves along with it to the bottom. In the dark of night, the British heard wails and screams, but by the time they boarded the Brillante, no slaves were left on board and Homans went free.

The British law was changed in 1839 to allow a vessel to be seized if there was proof it had once carried slaves, such as the presence of a slave deck, chains and shackles, or even hatches with open gratings. Actual slaves on board were no longer necessary as evidence of a slaver.

Despite many captures by British ships, the illegal trade increased as more and more slave ships sailed under the protection of the American flag. The United States refused to allow its ships to be stopped and boarded by the British. "American citizens prosecuting a lawful commerce in the African seas under the flag of their country are not responsible for the abuses or unlawful use of that flag by others," stated President John Tyler in 1841. If slave ships were approached by other American vessels, they would immediately hoist the Spanish or Portuguese flag and often carried documents from those particular countries to back them up.

By the 1850s, the American government was making more of an effort to stop the illegal slave trade and American ships joined the British in patrolling the Atlantic. In 1860, the *Erie*, captained by Nathaniel Gordon, was seized with a cargo of 890 slaves en route from the Congo to the island of Cuba. The slaves were released in Liberia, Africa, and Gordon was taken to New York to stand trial as a pirate under the 1820 law which made slave trading an act of piracy.

After one mistrial, Gordon was found guilty and sentenced to death. President Abraham Lincoln ignored a request for clemency and Gordon was executed on February 21, 1862, the only American slave ship captain to meet such a fate.

In 1850, Brazil made slave trading an act of piracy and also began to cooperate with the British in enforcement. Although the illegal trade from Africa all but ended by 1860, slavery still existed in the American South, Cuba, and Brazil.

With the Emancipation Proclamation in 1863 and the passage of the 13th Amendment to the Constitution in 1865, slavery was finally and totally eliminated in America. Cuba and Brazil freed their existing slaves in 1886 and 1888, respectively.

The Atlantic slave trade had come to an end, after nearly 400 years.

An Act for the Abolition of the Slave Trade

(Donnan, Ibid, *Volume II*, pp. 659-660).

...Be it therefore enacted by the King's most Excellent Majesty, by and with the Advice and Consent of the Lords Spiritual and Temporal, and Commons, in this present Parliament assembled, and by the Authority of the same, That from and after the First Day of May One thousand eight hundred and seven, the African Slave Trade, and all and all manner of dealing and trading in the Purchase, Sale, Barter, or Transfer of Slaves, or of Persons intended to be sold, transferred, used, or dealt with as Slaves, practised and carried on, in, at, to or from any Part of the Coast or Countries of Africa, shall be, and the same is hereby utterly abolished, prohibited, and declared to be unlawful; and also that all and all manner of dealing, either by way of Purchase, Sale, Barter, or Transfer, or by means of any other Contract or Agreement whatever, relating to any Slaves, or to any Persons intended to be used or dealt with as Slaves, for the Purpose of such Slaves or Persons being removed and transported either immediately or by Transhipment at Sea or otherwise, directly or indirectly from Africa, or from any Island, Country, Territory, or Place whatever, in the West Indies, or in any other Part of America, not being in the Dominion, Possession, or Occupation of His Majesty, to any other Island, Country, Territory or Place whatever, is hereby in like Manner utterly abolished, prohibited, and declared to be unlawful...

Act to Prohibit the Importation of Slaves into the United States, 1807

(Donnan, Ibid, *Volume IV*, p. 666).

An Act to prohibit the importation of Slaves into any port or place within the jurisdiction of the United States, from and after the first day of January, in the year of our Lord one thousand eight hundred and eight.

Be it enacted by the Senate and House of Representatives of the United States of America in Congress assembled, That from and after the first day of January, one thousand eight hundred and eight, it shall not be lawful to import or bring into the United States or the territories thereof from any foreign kingdom, place, or country, any negro, mulatto, or person of colour, with intent to hold, sell, or dispose of such negro, mulatto, or person of colour, as a slave, or to be held to service or labour...

When slavery was abolished in 1865, taverns and storefronts which had been the site of slave auctions for so many years in the American colonies removed their shingles advertising the sale of slaves. The photo above depicts Whitehall Street in Atlanta, Georgia in 1864.

A Slaver's Log Book or 20 Years Residence in Africa

by Captain Theophilus Conneau

(Conneau, Ibid, pp. 87-88).

March, 1827 The landing of slaves [during the illegal trade] is generally made now on some given point of the coast where the absence of habitation is apparent, but some hidden hut denotes the spot of the persons appointed to await the arrival. As soon as the anchor is let go, one or more boats are sent off and the landing is effected while some of the crew dismantle the vessel in order to avoid notice from inland or in the offing.

53

Once the cargo is landed, it is hastened in the Interior as soon as possible, escorted by the Captain and part of the crew all well armed, and made to walk at a rapid rate. In this manner they are conducted to the nearest plantation whose consent is purchased before, and there deposited, which secures them from the grasping power of the petty magistrate of the district...who in imitation of his superior the Governor would exact a remuneration for his consent.

In the meantime, a dispatch is sent to the owners in Havana, Matanzas, or Santiago de Cuba, who arrive post haste at the plantation with coarse dresses for the new-arrived Africans and the necessary gold to pay off the crew.

Messengers are sent off to the different slave brokers, who inform the needy purchaser that a quantity of...slaves are to be disposed, mentioning the nation but not the owner, Captain, or the vessel that landed them. As gold is expected, nothing is said of the terms.

The vessel, if small, is either dismantled or so disfigured as to warrant a safe return in a port of clearance with a cargo of sugar or molasses and under the coasting flag. But if the vessel is a brig or rigged ship, she is either burnt or sunk. Sometimes she is sent to St. Thomas, Curacao, or Spanish San Domingo as a distressed vessel, to appear again perhaps transmuted under another rig, paint, and name.

On the arrival of the slaves in a plantation, they are well fed with fresh provisions and abundance of fruit, which greatly astonishes the African who in his joy forgets his country, friends, and relations...

Poems on the Abolition of the Slave Trade

(From James Montgomery, James Grahame, and E. Benger, *Poems on the Abolition of the Slave Trade*. New York: Garland Publishing, Inc., 1978, p. 1, originally published in 1809).

'Thy chains are broken, Africa, be free!'

Thus saith the island-empress of the sea;

Thus saith Britannia. — O ye winds and waves!

Waft the glad tidings to the land of slaves;

Proclaim on Guinea's coast, by Gambia's side,

And far as Niger rolls his eastern tide

Through radiant realms beneath the burning zone,

Where Europe's curse is felt, her name unknown,

'Thus saith Britannia, empress of the sea,

'Thy Chains are broken, Africa, be free!'

Effects of the Slave Trade

Historians disagree as to the total number of slaves actually imported from Africa during the period of the Atlantic trade. Estimates range from a low of 3 1/2 million to a high of 25 million people. According to Curtin in *The Atlantic Slave Trade*, approximately 10 million Africans were taken from their homeland, with the United States receiving only a small portion of the total, about five percent.

South America received 49.2% of all imported slaves with Brazil getting the lion's share of 38.1%. The Caribbean Islands received 42.2% with Haiti, Jamaica, and Cuba getting the largest numbers.

A Speculative Geographical Distribution of Slave Imports During the Whole Period of the Atlantic Slave Trade

(Curtin, Ibid, parts of pp. 88-89).

Region and Country	No.	%
Grand Total	9,566,000	100.0
North America	651,000	6.8
Territory of the United States	427,000	4.5
Mexico and Central America	224,000	2.3
Caribbean Islands	4,040,000	42.2
Haiti	864,000	9.0
Cuba	702,000	7.3
Jamaica	748,000	7.8
Leeward Islands	346,000	3.6
Martinique	366,000	3.8
Barbados	387,000	4.0
Others	627,000	6.7
South America	4,700,000	49.2
The Guianas	531,000	5.6
Brazil	3,647,000	38.1
Spanish South America	522,000	5.5

By 1800, a little over one million blacks lived in the United States. By 1850, that number more than tripled. In America the black population increased naturally due to high birth and fertility rates. The illegal trade accounted for only a very small portion of the increase.

This population expansion in America contrasted greatly with the Caribbean Islands and South America, where slave populations decreased each year. It is believed that climate, tropical diseases, and hard labor connected with growing certain crops, combined to influence the rate of natural increase or decrease of slaves.

As a system of labor, the slave trade stimulated the economic development of Europe, America, and the New World colonies. Yet, it fostered such deep-seated racism and prejudice that the aftereffects are felt by all, even today.

According to John Woolman in *Some Considerations on the Keeping of Negroes*, "Placing on Men the...Title SLAVE, dressing them in uncomely Garments, keeping them to servile Labour, in which they are often dirty, tends gradually to fix a Notion in the Mind, that they are a Sort of People below us in Nature, and leads us to consider them as such in all our Conclusions about them..."

As slaves, the Africans lost their freedom. As blacks, their skin color set them apart from others. In the eyes of many whites, these two factors resulted in the slave's loss of humanity. Blacks came to be thought of as inferior creatures, not regular human beings. Plantation owners came to believe that blacks were born to serve and that was their role in society. This was how they justified their increasing demands for slave labor.

"That nameless Dutch vessel which arrived a year before the *Mayflower*...carried not only twenty Negroes but, for the future, everything those Negroes and their successors would contribute to American wealth and culture," summed up Daniel P. Mannix in his book *Black Cargoes*, "including Carolina rice...and the

Cotton Kingdom. She carried...the maritime trade of New England and the training of the first sailors in the United States Navy; then the plantation system, the Abolition Society, the Missouri Compromise, and the Civil War; then Reconstruction, the Solid South, Jim Crow, and the struggle for integration. She carried the spirituals, jazz, the researches of such Negro scientists as George Washington Carver, the contributions to American culture of younger Negro musicians, statesmen, scholars, and writers; and she also carried, for this age of international struggles, the first link between the United States and Africa."

Through the years, the black population of the United States has grown and developed into an important and productive segment of the national community. Afro-Americans have made significant contributions in government, politics, the arts and sciences, sports, and music, influencing each and every facet of our American life.

Suggested Further Reading

* Major sources of excerpts in this book are listed at the beginning of each selection and are also recommended as Further Reading.

* Clarkson, Thomas. *The History of the Abolition of the African Slave Trade — Volumes I and II.* London: Frank Cass & Company Limited, 1968, originally published in 1808.

* Conneau, Captain Theophilus. *A Slaver's Log Book or 20 Years Residence in Africa.* Englewood Cliffs, New Jersey: Prentice Hall, Inc., 1976, originally published in 1854.

* Cowley, Malcolm. *Adventures of an African Slaver.* New York: Albert & Charles Boni, 1928.

* Curtin, Philip D. *The Atlantic Slave Trade.* Madison, Wisconsin: The University of Wisconsin Press, 1969.

* Donnan, Elizabeth. *Documents Illustrative of the History of the Slave Trade to America — Volume I — 1441-1700, Volume II— The 18th Century, Volume III — New England and the Middle Colonies, Volume IV — The Border Colonies and the Southern Colonies.* New York: Octagon Books Inc., 1965, originally published in 1930, 1931, 1932 and 1935 respectively.

* Dow, George Francis. *Slave Ships and Slaving.* Salem, Massachusetts: Marine Research Society, 1927.

Hawkins, Joseph. *A History of a Voyage to the Coast of Africa.* Northbrook, Illinois: Metro Books, Inc., 1972.

Inikori, Joseph E. and Stanley L. Engerman, Editors. *The Atlantic Slave Trade.* Durham, South Carolina: Duke University Press, 1992.

Jordan, Winthrop D. *White Over Black.* Chapel Hill, North Carolina: The University of North Carolina Press, 1968.

Jones, Howard. *Mutiny on the Amistad: The Saga of a Slave Revolt and Its Impact on American Abolition, Law, and Diplomacy.* New York: Oxford University Press, 1987.

Kaplan, Sidney. *The Black Presence in the Era of the American Revolution, 1770-1800.* Washington, DC: New York – Geographic Society Ltd., in association with Smithsonian Institution Press, 1978.

Killingray, David. *The Slave Trade.* St. Paul, Minnesota: Greenhaven Press, Inc., 1980.

* Kolchin, Peter. *American Slavery 1619-1877.* New York: Hill and Wang, 1993.

* Mannix, Daniel P. *Black Cargoes.* New York: Viking Press, 1962.

* Montgomery, James, James Grahame and E. Benger. *Poems on the Abolition of the Slave Trade.* New York: Garland Publishing, Inc., 1978, originally published in 1809.

* Owen, Nicholas. *Journal of a Slave-Dealer.* London: George Routledge and Sons, Ltd., 1930.

* Pope-Hennessy, James. *Sins of the Fathers.* New York: Alfred A. Knopf, 1968.

* Rawley, James A. *The Transatlantic Slave Trade.* New York: W.W. Norton & Company, 1981.

The Connecticut Scholar, Number 10. *The Amistad Incident: Four Perspectives.* Middletoan, Conn: Connecticut Humanities Council, 1992.

Wedderburn, Robert. *The Horrors of Slavery and Other Writings.* New York: Markus Weiner Publishing, 1991, originally published in 1824.

Woolman, John. *Some Considerations on the Keeping of Negroes.* New York: Grossman Publishers, 1976, originally published in 1754.

Yates, Elizabeth. *Amos Fortune: Free Man.* New York: Puffin Books, 1989. (Young Adult)

About the Editor

Phyllis Raybin Emert has a B.A. degree in Political Science-from the State University of New York at Stony Brook and an M.A. degree in Political Science/Public Administration from Penn State.

A free lance writer for nearly twenty years, she has thirty-two books published on a variety of subjects—from airplanes, animals, and automobiles, to pretzels, sports heroes, and unsolved mysteries. Ms. Emert has edited two other titles in the Discovery Enterprises, Ltd.'s Perspectives on History Series —*Women in the Civil War: Warriors, Patriots, Nurses, and Spies,* and *All That Glitters: The Men and Women of the Gold and Silver Rushes.*

The Perspectives on History Series

CPSIA information can be obtained at www.ICGtesting.com
Printed in the USA
BVOW06s1929041115

425758BV00017B/91/P

9 781878 668486